Andrew & Ashley's
EUROPEAN TOURS

KIDS' CULTURAL TRAVEL GUIDE TO PARIS WITH ACTIVITY BOOK AND TRAVEL JOURNAL

THIS BOOK BELONGS TO

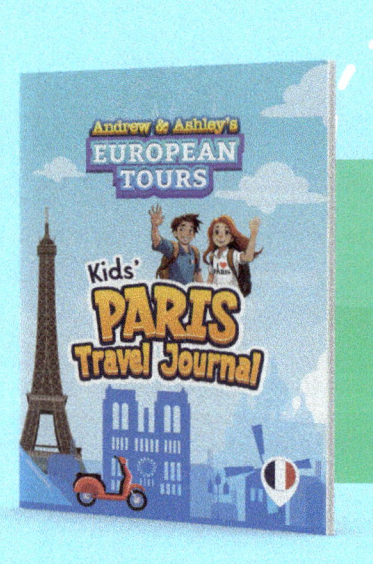

KEEP A JOURNAL OF YOUR EXPERIENCES IN PARIS TO SHARE WITH FRIENDS AND FAMILY WHEN YOU RETURN.

Get the *Paris Travel Journal* here.

HERE'S WHAT WE'RE UP TO ON THIS TRIP!

Hi, my name is Ashley. My twin brother Andrew and I can't wait to share what we've learned and take you on a tour of Paris' most popular attractions for kids like us. This town is rich in tourist sites with old and new culture! So cool.

The great thing about being in Paris, France is it is such a beautiful city filled with amazing architecture and people. Just about everywhere you go is a feast for the eyes. Grand palaces and chateaus, a park for kids where you can sail small boats, people sitting outside at sidewalk cafes eating croissants (so good!), and people playing music or selling their art in the streets. And don't forget Disneyland Paris is not far away either!

The French speak French — go figure — so we're going to introduce you to some easy words and phrases that you can try while you're there. Parlez-vous français? (That means do you speak French?) Don't worry, we'll tell you how to say it!

We've got some fun puzzles, activities, and even a trip planner to help you organize what you want to see with your family. If you're really on top of things, you'll buy tickets ahead to skip the long lines too.

But first a little about where you're going and what we'll do...

- Things to know about Paris and France
- How we'll get around to discover all the cool stuff
- Let's tour Paris!
- Test your knowledge
- Plan your trip

Get your passports ready to be stamped and welcome to Paris!

The Continent and Countries of Europe

Where in the world are France and Paris?

There are seven continents in the world, and Europe is one of them. Check out the map below to find the continent you live on.

ARCTIC OCEAN

EUROPE

ASIA

NORTH AMERICA

ATLANTIC OCEAN

PACIFIC OCEAN

PACIFIC OCEAN

AFRICA

SOUTH AMERICA

INDIAN OCEAN

AUSTRALIA

ANTARCTICA

Travel
PASSPORT
PARIS

Europe is made up of four geographic areas. If we visited each of those areas, we'd see that the culture-things like food, art, music, and interests, can sometimes be similar within each of the regions. Join me on this tour to find out more!

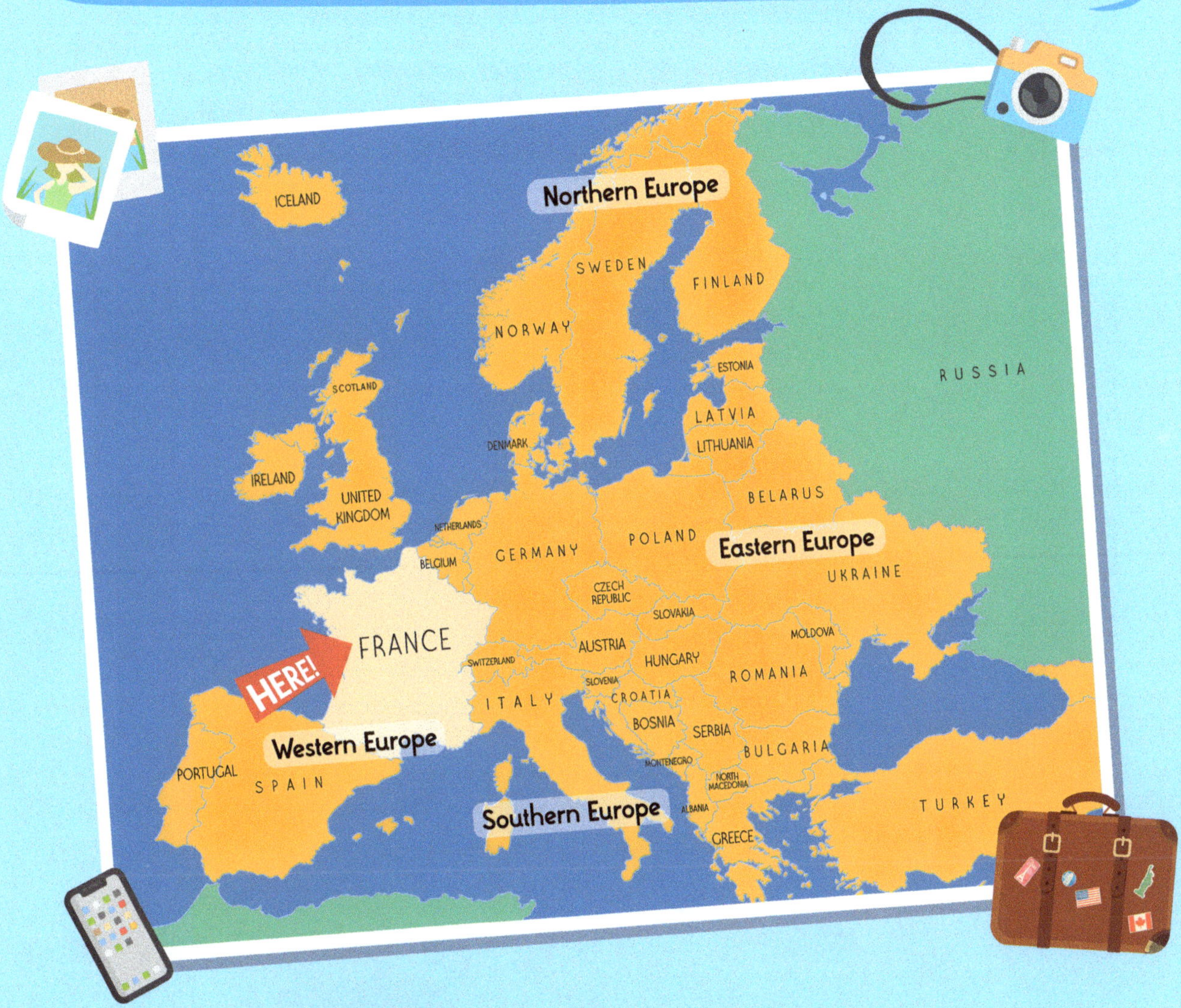

ICELAND

Northern Europe

SWEDEN

FINLAND

NORWAY

ESTONIA

RUSSIA

SCOTLAND

LATVIA

LITHUANIA

DENMARK

IRELAND

BELARUS

UNITED KINGDOM

NETHERLANDS

GERMANY

POLAND

Eastern Europe

BELGIUM

UKRAINE

CZECH REPUBLIC

HERE!

FRANCE

SLOVAKIA

MOLDOVA

SWITZERLAND

AUSTRIA

HUNGARY

SLOVENIA

ROMANIA

CROATIA

ITALY

BOSNIA

SERBIA

Western Europe

MONTENEGRO

BULGARIA

PORTUGAL

NORTH MACEDONIA

SPAIN

ALBANIA

TURKEY

Southern Europe

GREECE

DID YOU KNOW? There are 51 countries that make up Europe.

The Country of France & City of Paris

There is so much more to discover in France, but we're going to focus on our favorite cool stuff in Paris on this tour — France's capital city!

First of all, France is in mainland Europe. So the way to get into the country is to fly by airplane or take a train from another country you're visiting. Flights from other continents can be long, so don't forget this book and the Paris travel journal too so you have something fun to do!

France is a land of enchantment and history! Established in the 5th century, France is a country full of culture and charm. Nestled in the heart of Europe, it shares borders with Belgium, Luxembourg, Germany, Switzerland, Italy, Spain, Monaco, and Andorra. Each region is a treasure trove of unique experiences — from the romantic streets of Paris to the sun-soaked vineyards of Bordeaux. The Loire Valley boasts fairytale castles, while the French Riviera beckons with azure (blue) beaches. Alpine wonders await in the French Alps, and the picturesque Provence is a canvas of lavender fields. France is a feast for the senses, promising delectable cuisine, timeless art, and unforgettable adventures for young explorers!

THIS IS THE REGION WE WILL BE EXPLORING ON THIS TOUR.

LILLE

PARIS

STRASBOURG

NANTES

LYON

BORDEAUX

TOULOUSE

MONTPELLIER

MARSEILLE

NICE

AJACCIO

Fun Facts About France & Paris

DID YOU KNOW?

- France was established as a nation in the 1400s AD (over 600 years ago)

- France has a population of 67 million, similar to the UK but France has 73% more land

- Geographically speaking, France is 342,807 square miles in size whereas the UK is 94,000 square miles. Texas in the United States has about 368,500 square miles

- The largest city in France, Paris, has a population of around 2.1 million people — that means 64 million people (a lot) are spread out over a very big country

- France used to have kings that ruled the country. The last emperor to rule the country from 1852 to 1870 was Napoleon III, or Charles-Louis-Napoléon Bonaparte. You can learn more about him when you visit Paris museums. He is world famous

- Official language: French. Bonjour! (pronounced "bon-juer" and it means good day or hello!)

- The city of Paris was established in the 1200s AD (over 800 years ago)

- An international city, you may also hear English, German, Italian, Portuguese, Arabic or Chinese too

- Today the country of France makes money from exporting products like pharmaceuticals (medicine), aircraft, cars, and food products like cheese!

- The Luxor Obelisk is the oldest object in Paris. It was gifted to France in 1829 by Muhammad Ali Pasha of Egypt. It is over 3200 years old. Can you find it on the map?

Wait, what? That's old! The US was founded over 200 years ago, France over 600 years ago... and the Obelisk was originally built around 3300 years ago in Egypt! Note to self: must visit Egypt one day!

CULTURE ALERT

FLAGS OF FRANCE

FRANCE!

You'll see mostly the French flag but also the European Union (EU) flag. France is a founding member of the EU. You may hear adults talking about it. It's basically a union of European countries that govern together to be stronger together (most countries in Europe are smaller in size compared to Australia and the US for example).

CULTURE ALERT

A common French saying is **planter un drapeau** which means 'to plant a flag'. According to the dictionary Trésor de la langue française, it means 'to be the first to publicly express an opinion, to take a position.'

The flag, on the one hand, is a symbol of belonging (to a nation). To plant one's flag would mean to express belonging. Today, it's not uncommon to see a political protest in Paris with people showing that they are taking a position for an important cause.

Another saying: **mettre son drapeau dans sa poche** literally means 'to put your flag in your pocket.' This expression is said to mean to hide your views and/or beliefs. You'll have to use your French translation app to find out how to say that one!

OO-AAA-O

EUROPEAN UNION FLAG

You'll likely see this flag on license plates around France as well as in EU countries.

DID YOU KNOW? The old French flag has fleur-de-lis (or flower of the lily) symbols on it. Keep your eyes peeled because you'll see the fleur-de-lis symbol in many other places like on decorations for the home.

Fun Facts About France & Paris

FRENCH GOVERNMENT

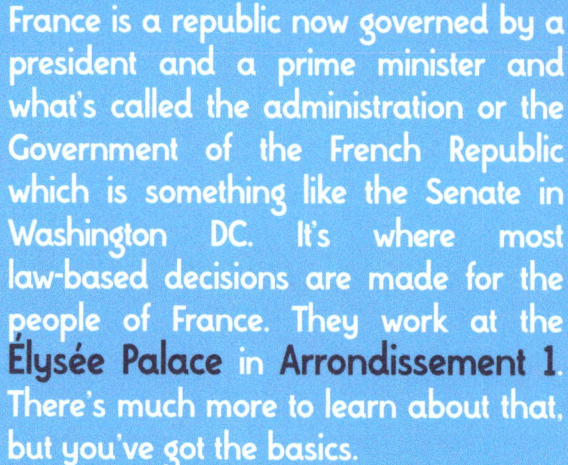

France is a republic now governed by a president and a prime minister and what's called the administration or the Government of the French Republic which is something like the Senate in Washington DC. It's where most law-based decisions are made for the people of France. They work at the **Élysée Palace** in Arrondissement 1. There's much more to learn about that, but you've got the basics.

As you've learned, France no longer has a royal family but there are still thousands of French citizens who have titles and can trace their family back to nobility. There are also many castles and chateaus around the country. We hope you'll get time to see them!

FUN FACTS!

Have you ever heard of a **court jester**? The French government used to employ them to entertain people during royal court sessions, and some say they were advisors too. They were also traveling performers at fairs and town markets. You can still see them today at some street fairs in France.

You'll see France's royal families represented in paintings in museums. Their clothing was very fancy. Here's **King Louis XIV** for example! He lived in the Palace of Versailles just outside central Paris and was a famous supporter of the arts. You can tour this beautiful palace to learn more!

SCHOOLS & UNIVERSITIES

There are some famous schools and universities in Paris that you may have heard about or seen in the movies — with students from all around the world. So study hard and learn French in school if you want to go there someday.

- Sorbonne University
- École des Ponts ParisTech
- Institute Polytechnique de Paris
- Université de Paris

Fun Facts About France & Paris

DID YOU KNOW?

SO MANY CHATEAUS. WHY?

There are over **40,000 chateaus** (a castle or mansion) in France. Some are restored to their original glory and some are ruins. That's a LOT of castles! To compare, the UK has 4,000. You may ask yourself why are there so many? They were built between 900s AD and 1900s AD (that's between 100 and 1100 years ago!) and many were built for kings and queens who battled for power over local armies and royal families. Territories were much smaller back then. Imagine, if you travel outside of Paris, it will be difficult to NOT see one! And sometimes you can stay overnight in a chateau — some are hotels!

That's a LOT of chateaus!

Every red dot represents a chateau!

You'll see so many amazing older buildings and castles in Paris. The US was first established in 1776 — that's over 300 years later than France. They built some amazing architecture back in that day. Read on to find out.

The most impressive chateau in France is the **Palace of Versailles** — you can visit it in Paris on this tour!

How could so many kings and queens (nobles) back in medieval times afford to build so many castles? Money was passed down through families and it was typically gained from owning land with pastures, orchards, timberland, and hunting grounds. They charged peasants tax to live and farm on the land too.

DID YOU KNOW?

They didn't have banks back then so money was largely in gold and land. It was stored within rooms in castles where they lived. There must have been a lot of guards around. Ever seen a **French medieval coin**?

Fun Facts About France & Paris

CURRENCY

What type of money will I use in France?

France's currency is the Euro. The Euro symbol is €. And the coins are called cents (short for centimes).

Remember we mentioned earlier that there are 51 countries in Europe. Of those, 27 have become members of the European Union and they mostly use the same currency (and have the same license plate symbol too).

Bank notes (paper) come in €5, €10, €20, €50 and €100, €200, and €500.

Coins come in €1 and €2 euros, and 50, 20, 10, 5, 2, and 1 cent amounts. You might want to get some Euros and take a look at them before you go out so you can identify them faster when it's time to pay.

Parisian Culture

We are about to explore another culturally rich destination of the world. France's culture is unique and adored by many. Culture is the ideas, customs, and social behavior of a people or society. There is so much to cover, and we can't tell you about everything, but this will be your adventure. Agree visit as many museums, monuments, restaurants, or theaters and go on as many tours as you can! Learn for yourself what you love, like, or can do without.

Paris is called the **City of Lights** and the **City of Romance** for a reason! See if you can figure out why.

Let's start with some things you need to know or may notice right away.

Parisian Culture

♥ PARIS, FRANCE ♥

CULTURE ALERT

There is so much culture to share as Paris and France are famous in many categories. We'll just show you our favorites for kids and stuff you should be in the know about! We can't include them all. So before your trip to Paris, do your research! And be ready to learn more when you get there.

The next few pages include one big culture alert. You won't believe how Parisians express themselves in so many ways. It's never dull in Paris! There are always people getting together to enjoy the best that the city has to offer. Sometimes that's an event or a show, but most importantly to enjoy a **"laissez-faire"** lifestyle. Loosely translated it is to let things unfold naturally or easily — to enjoy the moment and go with the flow.

If you remember anything at all about French culture, remember this: French cuisine (cooking and food) is known around the world.

J'adore la cuisine française! ♥ That means: "I adore French food!" The tasting, eating, making, and sharing of food is the essence of culture in France. The French and especially Parisians love to go out and meet friends in bistros and boulangeries. Sunday afternoons are for dinner with family and friends. The French are very passionate about how food is made and how their animals are cared for too.

And it is not uncommon to see people lined 20+ out the door at a boulangerie on a Saturday morning. Why? Read on and you'll get what I mean...

But there is much more to the culture. Enjoy!

"DID YOU KNOW?"

What is a **bistro** you ask? A French bistro is typically a family-owned restaurant, passed down through generations, typically with a few tables inside and out, and a bar counter with seating. Traditionally, they serve small dishes that the cook decides to make that day depending on what's good at the market. It's a very casual setting. Sometimes the decor is very homey too. Typical dishes are **boeuf bourguignon** (basically beef stew) with a dessert like **tarte Tatin** (a small fruit tart). Almost every one of them has fries too!

You will want to pay attention to this one! On **Saturday mornings** especially, the French line up at the **boulangerie** (bakery) and **patisserie** (pastries) to pick up their daily bread, croissants, pies, and pastries. And WOW they are delicious. It's worth waiting in line!

La petite crêperie means a "small" place that serves crêpes! YUM!

Parisian Culture

FOOD & DRINK

Wine, champagne and some foods are among of the largest exported products for France. If you go to a mainstream grocery store in many countries you'll find it, or they'll attempt to make the food — but it may not be as good as it is in France!

- Quiche Lorraine — ham and cheese egg bake

- Omelette

- Croque-monsieur — cheesy ham sandwich

- Sandwich Jambon Beurre — basically a French baguette with the best tasting butter you've ever had with ham inside, sometimes cheese too

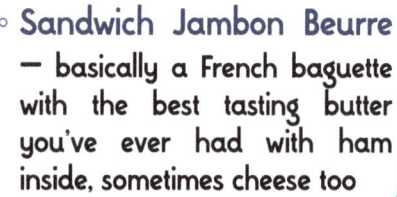

- Croque-madame is the same as the Croque-monsieur but with an egg on top!

- Crêpes are a very thin pancake but usually filled with either sweet things like fruit and chocolate, or savory things like ham and cheese. The combinations are endless! You'll find these on menus all over Paris but the official place that does mostly crêpe's is called a — you guessed it — a crêperie!

FUN FACTS!

Fries are not French. The debate continues but the story goes that the Belgians first introduced them to the public. Many Belgians speak French too, but that's another story.

FRENCH WINE & CHAMPAGNE

ORANGINA

MAIN DISHES

Ashley loves her French food — we just can't list it all here. You can also get seafood and shrimp, mussels galore. But watch out for the escargot! You'll either love it or not like it so much. It's snails!

CHARCUTERIE
(A PLATTER MEATS)

- Saucisson — dried French sausage
- Pâté — a meat spread to put on bread
- Jambon — dried thinly sliced ham

FRENCH CHEESE

- Comté is good in a sandwich
- Camembert
- Brie
- La Vache qui rit means the laughing cow. Kids like it!

La vache qui rit

FRENCH BREAD

- Baguette — a long, thin, crusty on the outside and soft and pillowy on the inside bread great for sandwiches, dipping in sauces and much more

FRENCH CHOCOLATE

Oh la la! Some of the best you'll ever taste

FRENCH PASTRIES & PIES

- Macarons

- Pain au chocolat

- Éclair

- Croissant

Parisian Culture

ARTISTS

There are too many world-famous artists to name here so you'll have to visit the museums to find out more. A great place to start is the **Louvre Museum** which shows some of the most famous art in the world — paintings that if you were to buy them it would cost millions! What is the most interesting, is these artists' life stories. Many of them knew each other in the 1800s in Paris during the impressionist period. They sat around in bistros (coffee shops with a little bit of food) talking, drinking, and learning from each other. Once you visit, you will be able to imagine how a warm sunny day in a park could inspire them to do such amazing work.

VINCENT VAN GOGH

∘ Famous painting "Starry Night."

 **TOULOUSE-LAUTREC**

SEURAT

 **DEGAS**

MATISSE

 **GAUGUIN**

CÉZANNE

CLAUDE MONET

∘ Famous painting "Bridge Over a Pond of Water Lilies."

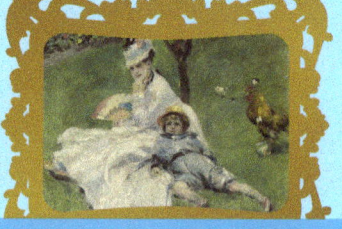

PIERRE AUGUSTE RENOIR

∘ Famous painting "Madame Monet and her son, 1864."

THEATRE

LES MISÉRABLES MUSICAL

- It means "the miserables" in English
- A very famous play running worldwide today written by a Frenchman from Paris named Victor Hugo.

MOULIN ROUGE MUSICAL

- The name means "red mill" in English and there is also a theatre of the same name in Paris.

You can visit the **Moulin Rouge theatre** in Paris. It still exists to this day. The musical is very famous and the stories from those days were also made into a movie released in 2001. It was about an adult theatre in the Bohemian period (1890s) with a poor poet who falls for a dancer who worked at Moulin Rouge theatre. They did a dance called the can-can. Perhaps you have heard of it?

STREET ART

- Ever heard of a **mime**? It's a person who does theatre on the street with a live audience. The mimes dress like this and don't talk, but follow someone on the street and mimic their movements. It's very French!
- You can take tours of the art on city streets but if you don't have time, be on the lookout whenever you're walking. The districts of Oberkampf, Belleville and Menilmontant are rich in street art.

Parisian Culture

BOOKS & MOVIES

Paris has always been a great source of inspiration for the movie industry. And many show the famous **Eiffel Tower**.

PUSS IN BOOTS

Originally, the book in French was called Le Chat Botte. You may know about his appearance in the 2022 animated film **Puss in Boots: The Last Wish** where he is voiced over by a very famous actor named **Antonio Banderas**!

TALES OF MOTHER GOOSE

Originally a French fairy tale character in a book collection by **Charles Perrault** in the 1700s. It was first translated in English and entitled Tales of Mother Goose.

THE THREE MUSKETEERS

The Three Musketeers was originally a novel written by French author **Alexandre Dumas**. It's about chivalrous swordsmen who fight for justice. The main character is a young man named **d'Artagnan**. He leaves home to travel to Paris hoping to join the Musketeers of the Guard. He doesn't get accepted right away but he finds three inseperables who then became d"Artagnan and The Three Musketeers named **Athos, Porthos and Aramis**.

THE LITTLE PRINCE

A prince's travels throughout outer space.

MOVIES TO WATCH BASED ON FRENCH BOOKS

Here are some books that also became movies to watch in English before you travel to Paris. Get a sense of what life was like in Paris.

1. Madeline
2. The Aristocats
3. The Three Musketeers
4. The Hunchback of Notre-Dame (Disney animated musical)

PARKS AND PLAYGROUNDS

Parisians love their parks. The kids play and the adults play things like petanques too. Jardin du Luxembourg (Luxembourg Garden) in Left Bank has fun stuff for kids.

MUSIC

CLASSICAL MUSIC

France has produced several prominent Romantic composers and the list is long of composers since the 2nd century (1100s BC). You could say that music is a very important part of French culture. Claude Debussy (August 22, 1862 – March 25, 1918) is one of the most famous.

LIVE MUSIC IN PARIS

Paris is a wonderful place to listen to live music. You may not be able to understand the words, but the music creates a mood that goes well with the surroundings. You can find musicians in the streets or a cafe in the summer just about any night of the week.

FAMOUS CHILDREN'S SONGS

Did you learn these songs in school? Frère Jacques and Alouette are world-famous songs that kids in France learn too. Chances are your parents know them.

Parisian Culture

MUSEUMS & AUCTIONS

MUSÉE DE LOUVRE

The most famous and the most grand museum of all has a dedicated family space called the Studio and an app for kids ages 7-11.

ATELIER DES LUMIÈRES

This "workshop of lights" shows Van Gogh's Starry Night paintings on huge walls — it's really cool. The story goes that he was having a difficult time in his life right before this was painted. Can you tell? Emotions sure can bring out amazing and creative things when it comes to art.

Some of the best museums in the world are to be found here in Paris. You could spend hours and days sorting through all of them. They house very famous, important paintings, sculptures and historical artifacts about the people who lived in the region long ago and the people they knew in far away lands.

Paris also has famous auction houses that sell very expensive artifacts to wealthy people for their collections. You may hear on the news about a painting selling for several hundred million Euros. And because of the high fashion nature of Paris, designer items like handbags are commonly sold at auction too. The most expensive ever sold was an **Hermès white crocodile Himalaya** handbag, encrusted with diamonds. It was bought for 340,000 Euros! What?!

FASHION & DESIGN

Paris design and fashion houses have had a big influence on what the world wears. These top designers shape the "haute couture" or high fashion for the world — and you can see their gorgeous stores (very expensive ball gowns and suits) mostly in the "Rive Gauche" or Left Bank. More on this later.

PARIS DESIGN & FASHION HOUSES

- Dior — perfume & clothing
- Chanel — perfume & clothing
- Louis Vuitton — clothing & accessories
- Hermès — handbags & accessories
- Givenchy — men's & women's clothing
- YSL or Yves Saint Laurent — men's & women's clothing & perfume

Once a year Paris puts on a big show called **Paris Fashion Week** where next seasons' fashion designs are revealed.

Parisian Culture

FRENCH SPORTS

Many people are passionate about sports in France. There are 167,000 sport clubs in France with 15 million members. Football is by far the most popular sport. If you plan to be in Paris for longer than a few days, take in one of the many sporting events held in stadiums throughout the Paris area.

FOOTBALL

- Ligue 1 is the professional association of football clubs. There are 20 teams in the club.
- Primary Paris teams are Paris Saint-Germain and Stade Francais Paris.

CYCLING

- The Tour de France is one of the world's top cycling events. It is broadcast on television in many languages.

RUGBY

- The Rugby Union was first introduced in the 1870s by British residents. It's mostly played in the south of France.

TENNIS

- Each year Paris hosts the French Open which is a major tennis tournament held at the Roland Garros in Paris typically starting in late May.

MOTORSPORTS

- If you watch Formula 1, you'll know that France is all in.
- The Le Mans race across France takes place in August.

BASKETBALL

- France's national basketball team competes internationally.

CULTURE ALERT

There are many more casual sports events enjoyed by the locals too.
- Ski racing
- Boules or pétanque
- Horse racing and dressage

Kylian Mbappe is ranked as France's Top 3 football (soccer) star player who plays for Paris Saint-Germain and the France national team. Kylian is one of the youngest and highest paid players in Ligue 1. He is known for being the team's all-time top goalscorer and ranks 9th for assists so far in League 1 history. Amazing for such a young guy!

PARIS IS HOSTING THE 2024 SUMMER OLYMPIC GAMES

Ashley and I love the Olympic Games! It inspires us to really pick a sport and to feel part of something bigger. This is an exciting summer in Paris, as they are hosting the 2024 Summer Games. According to the official website, there are 28 official sports being hosted this year. We've put together a guide and workbook for you, whether you're in Paris or watching on TV, this journal gets you up to speed with pages to record your top 5 favorite sports and all the winners. It includes a few stats and some interesting trivia too!

Get it here!

CULTURE ALERT

Jousting was a spectator sport back in the Renaissance times (1500s) in France when the players would wear a suit of armor to protect themselves and joust on a field with the royalty and the village spectators watching. You can find jousting demonstrations to this day in parts of France.

Parisian Culture

FRENCH LANGUAGE WORDS & PHRASES TO TRY

Bonjour!

Hi!

PARLEZ-VOUS ANGLAIS? DO YOU SPEAK ENGLISH?

Here are some easy words and phrases in French and English that you may want to try!

When you travel in Europe, almost every country you visit speaks a unique language. London speaks English, Italy speaks Italian, Germans speak German, France speaks French...and so on. It's not always the case though as languages can sometimes be shared across countries in a region, too. But not to worry, especially in a big city, you can always find someone who speaks English to help you. You will likely be visiting for a short time, so we'll keep this short and easy.

WHAT YOU'LL SEE, HEAR, SMELL, AND TASTE...

You're going to see, hear, smell, and taste a lot of new things, but you'll also be able to find some familiar things too. Don't worry, you will be able to speak English to ask questions in most public places like hotels and museums. Museums usually have tours in English or headphones you can wear that can be set on English. You might need to have a little patience when working things out.

Keep your eyes peeled in Paris. You'll be able to find some brands from the US and other countries that you recognize as this is an international city. France exports a lot of things to other countries too! Which ones did you find? Keep track of them in your travel journal!

Here are some easy words and phrases in French and English that you may want to try! Most people know enough English in Paris to help you.

FRENCH WORD	ENGLISH TRANSLATION	PRONUNCIATION
Parlez-vous anglais?	Do you speak English?	Par-lay-voo-an-glay?
Bonjour!	Hello!	Bon-juer!
Bonsoir!	Good evening!	Bon-swa!
Merci	Thank you	Mer-see
Je suis désolé	I am sorry	Je-swee-deh-so-lay
Excusez-moi	Excuse me	Ex-coo-zay-mwa
Je voudrais...	I would like...	Jeh-voo-dray
Je cherche cette addresse	I am looking for this address	Jeh-shersh-set-address
C'est combien?	How much is it?	Seh-combian?
Je m'appelle _____	My name is _____	Jem-appel _____
Comment ça va?	How are you?	Kommon-sa-va?
Bien merci.	Fine, thank you.	Be-on-mercee
A bientôt!	See you soon!	Ah-bee-en-toe!
Àu revoir	Goodbye	Oh-ree-vwa
S'il vous plaît	If you please	See-voo-play
Bonne journée	Have a good day	Bon-jor-nay
Bon week-end	Have a nice weekend	Bon-week (or bon-weekend)
J'adore Paris!	I adore / love Paris!	Ja-door-pah-ree
L'addition s'il vous plaît	The bill / check please	La-di-sion-see-voo-play
Chat	Cat	Shaa
Chien	Dog	Sheon
Oh la la!	Oh wow / oh yes!	Oo-la-la!
Magnifique!	Magnificent / amazing	Man-ee-feek
Coucou!	What a surprise!	Coo-coo!
Madame	Mrs	Ma-dam
Monsieur	Mr	Miss-yeu
Mademoiselle	Miss	Maam-wa-zell
Petit	Small	Peu-tee
Grand	Big	Gran

Coucou!

Have some fun listening to all the different accents. Do you know what an accent is? When the French speak English the way they'll say it might not be exactly how you say it. So listen carefully and think about what they're trying to say to be a good communicator.

Paris Tour

Hi, it's Andrew, Ashley's twin brother. Welcome to Paris! There is so much to see and do, so we'll only feature our favorite things on this trip. One of my favorites is that Paris is a very international city. So you'll also see and meet people who live here who are originally from many different countries.

Other than that, you are going to see, hear, smell, taste, and experience a lot of new things. But don't worry, we've done it before and, trust me, you're going to like it! Spend a little time to take it all in at first.

CULTURE ALERT

When French people greet each other, they will say "bonjour!" or "bonsoir!" and then instead of hugging, it is tradition to give each other a light kiss on either cheek. Yes, even the men and boys. Did you know that? As a tourist, you don't have to do it... but you can if you want!

DID YOU KNOW?

The Louvre Museum is the most visited museum in the world. It has over a million visitors a year and the famous Mona Lisa painting is there on display. (I'll let you learn about that when you get there). The museum has over 460,000 pieces of art. That means, if you were take 30 seconds to view each item, that would take you 35 days. Don't worry, they've got things prioritized for you to see only the best first. But have a look at their website ahead of time to think about what you want to see.

ANDREW'S IN THE KNOW LIST

Here's a short list of some things you'll want to know upfront:

Official language:	• French
What people in Paris refer to themselves as:	• Parisians
My favorite French words:	• "Bonjour!" You can say it with energy to anyone when you walk in the door of the hotel, or a shop. They'll stay it back 😊 You can say it up to about 6 pm, then say "Bonsoir!"
Most likely place to have lunch:	• A bistro!
Our favorite things to eat:	• Ashley likes just about anything from the boulangerie, but her favorite is the pain au chocolat. I'll take anything in a crèpe, s'il vous plait!
Famous drink:	• Wine! I'll stick to Orangina or milk please!
Famous products:	• Cheese, pastries, chocolate!
What to wear:	• Summers in France are pretty warm, so bring shorts or a dress with comfortable walking shoes, a hat, and sunglasses. You'll be walking a lot. Dress casually but stylish to go out to dinner.
How to get around:	• Someone in your group needs to have a mobile phone with GPS! Plan ahead and be organized. Get tickets online well ahead of time. Otherwise, you'll get stuck standing in line, a LOT.
Paris is known for high fashion:	• Be on the lookout for models and well-dressed people!

ARRÊT STOP

FUN FACTS! There is only one stop sign in all of Paris. How is that possible? There is a system in place and the person on the right gets priority. That's it. The Arc du Triomphe is famous for its chaotic roundabout that exits to 5 roads. You've got to be brave to drive through there!

Look and listen to the world around you. Ashley likes the Louvre museum and Montmartre — which is a very artsy part of town. And I'm a big sports fan, so I'm more likely to choose a professional football (soccer) game. I also had a great time at the chocolate factory! Read on and find your favorites! Then plan your trip with your family on pages 56 to 58.

Paris Tour

Your flight to Paris may be a very long one. It may be overnight — so pack some comfortable travel clothes and this book to keep yourself entertained! It could be a short flight or train journey to Paris if you're already in Europe. Either way, you'll get some downtime to do the activities in this book and write in your Paris Travel Journal.

Once you arrive in Paris, you'll find that public transportation is easy but a bit chaotic. It's a busy city with taxis, bicycles, and cars all around. But don't worry, if you get orgnaized before you go, it will be fun.

The PARIS underground system is called **The Paris Metro** symbolized by an "M." Or sometimes it is just a small old-fashioned sign that says **Metro**. If you get to Paris central via Charles de Gualle airport, you can take the Metro directly from the airport — or a taxi of course, but there could be traffic jams which will make it a much longer trip. If you come to Paris via the train, you'll likely arrive at a main train station called **Paris Gare du Nord** where the Eurostar (inter-country) trains start and end their journeys.

Plan ahead to buy tickets during busy times and consider getting a **Navigo app or card** so you don't have to stop to buy tickets every time you use public transportation. This card allows you to add credit to it, so you can ride The Metro until the money runs out. Then you can add more money. Some attendants in the train station speak limited English but everything you need to know is online. Study the train map before you head out. The travel routes are color-coded, so it may take some thinking to plan your journey. You can always search on the internet in a GPS app for your destination, then press the little cable car icon and it will tell you which trains, buses, or underground to take.

Paris is divided into **arrondissements** or districts. Know in which arrondissement your hotel is, then find the arrondissement where your tour is, then find the closest Metro stop. **The River Seine** runs through the city and is a good landmark to help you know where you are in the city too. Anything left of the river is called **Left Bank** in English — which means it's on the left of the bank of the river.

DID YOU KNOW?

It's always good to have the name of your hotel to help you get back after a fun day of travel.

In the west **Neuilly, Boulogne, Saint Cloud, Levallois,** and **Versailles** are the most desired places to live in Paris.

PALAIS DE CONGRESS
18 MONTMARTRE
19 PARC DE LA VILLETTE
17
OPERA, PIGALLE
10
9
CANA, ST. MARTIN
8 CHAMPS-ELYSES
BOURSE
2
3 BASTILLE
BELLEVILLE, PERE-LACHAISE
LOUVRE 1
PICASSO MUSEUM
11
16 TROCADERO
7 EIFFEL TOWER
NOTRE DAME
4
20
6 SAINT GERMAIN
5 LATIN QUARTE
12 BERCY
15 PARC DES EXPOSITIONS
14 MONTPARNASSE
13 PLACE D'ITALIE

Paris Tour

We're going to suggest a potential plan for you, putting places together that are in the same areas. You're going to want to be very organized ahead of time, so use the planning section of this book to plot your trip. Make sure you organize yourselves with enough time to see things including travel time. And you've got to eat! It's a fully packed schedule so get ready and eat breakfast before you leave your hotel. This is the one time you'll regret not planning ahead to maximize your time. You can lie around to play games when you get home!

Purchase tickets well ahead of your visit so you can avoid the lines which could take an hour or more. The risk you take is that you don't get in at all after the long wait in line!

TRAVEL TIPS

 ## Top 10 cool things to see and experience

 • Eiffel Tower   • Sacre Coeur

• Arc de Triomphe   • Palace of Versaille

 • Notre Dame   • Arènes de Lutèce

 • Louvre Museum   • Catacombs

 • River Cruise   • Moulin Rouge

TRAVEL TIPS

Go online ahead of your trip to read about the different packages you can purchase when touring Paris. For example, you can buy tickets to get into the Louvre and book a tour, but it's not just for kids. Search online for tour companies that do special tours for kids. We did one that is a treasure hunt inside the Louvre museum! It was a super FUN way to hear stories that made it interesting for us.

LET'S TOUR PARIS!

You may not want to fill every morning and afternoon with tours, although it's nice to see as much as you can while you're there. Use the trip planner on pages 56 to 58 to first plot the tours that you can confirm with reservations. Then fill in the others.

DAY 1

TRAVEL DAY, KEEP MOVING SO YOU DON'T GET JET LAG!

If you just got to town after a long plane ride, get settled in your hotel and choose something to do in the afternoon or evening to help you to stay awake. Maybe go for a walk in a city park, or take a boat ride on the River Seine (pronounced "sen" just like like ten).

Day 1 Option: If you don't get in too late, you could take the Metro to catch an amazing view of Paris before sunset on top of Montmartre Hill at Sacre Coeur. You won't believe how huge Paris is from up there. There are buildings as far as the eye can see and you'll also be able to spot the Eiffel Tower too. Might be a good idea to have dinner in the Montmartre district afterward. It's close by.

○ **Bascilica Sacre Coeur de Montmartre**

- The Sacre Coeur is at the top of Montmartre Hill and is the second highest point in Paris. What's the highest point in Paris you ask? The Eiffel Tower of course — which you can also go to the top.
- The Sacre Coeur is home to the largest bell in France
- It took 39 years to build it, but it's not as old as you think. It was built after the Eiffel Tower and finished construction in 1914.

FUN FACTS!

What is a monument?
A monument is a statue, building or other structure put in place to memorialize a person or event. HINT: they are usually also monumental or large in size. 😄

Paris Tour

DAY 2

GET OUT TO SEE THE CITY AND ITS FAMOUS MONUMENTS!

It's going to be a busy day. Check the weather, then put on your walking shoes, sun glasses and sun screen. These monument structures are not just historical, they are incredible to see! They are very big and world famous. Imagine what it took hundreds of years ago to build them without automobiles and the equipment we use today.

- **MORNING:** Tuileries Gardens, Luxor Obelisk, Champs-Élysées, Arc de Triomphe
- **AFTERNOON:** Eiffel Tower & Aquarium de Paris

STOP #1

Morning: START AT THE TUILERIES GARDENS AND FIND THE LUXOR OBELEISK

You learned about the age of the Obelisk earlier in this book. Do you remember where it's from and why it's there? It's the oldest object in Paris and gifted to the city by an important person. Back in that day the Tuileries Palace is where royalty lived — but no longer. Now there's a park in its place. Surrounding you are hotels and offices of some sophisticated Parisians. You can see the Arc de Triomphe in the distance. Walk in that direction.

STOP #2

WALK VIA THE CHAMPES ÉLYSÉES TOWARD THE ARC DE TRIOMPH

Back in the day this was a grand royal promenade on horseback and carriage. Today it's a busy street lined with cafes with outdoor seating, and famous brand stores. Continue walking toward the Arc de Triomphe to witness something also grand, a bit hectic and unique.

STOP #3

ARC DE TRIOMPHE MEANS "ARCH OF VICTORY" IN ENGLISH

A famous monument in Paris at the center of the Place Charles de Gaulle. You may recognize that the largest airport you probably arrived to is of the same name. The Arc de Triomphe honors those who fought and died for France during the French revolution and the Napoleonic wars (there's that famous guy Napoleon's name again). You can see names of the French victories and generals inscribed on its inner and outer surfaces — that is if you can get near it.

This intersection is one of the busiest in Paris. It's a roundabout and we think normal traffic rules don't apply! See if you can figure out how cars get in and out of there and let us know!

Afternoon: COULD BE A GOOD POINT TO STOP FOR LUNCH

AQUARIUM DE PARIS **STOP #4**

SHARKS! We love this aquarium. Here are 8 reasons to love it too:

- 7500 fish
- 50 species of jellyfish
- 400 colonies of coral
- 40 sharks!
- Animated characters in the shows
- Mermaids!

Paris Tour

STOP #5 EIFFEL TOWER

Want to know why Paris is called the City of Lights? One of the reasons is that the Eiffel Tower is lit up at night with over 20,000 light bulbs! It's probably best to tour the Eiffel Tower during the day so you can see some of the other monuments from 984 feet up at the top. There is an observation deck that you can't miss and you'll be happy to know there is an elevator. 😄

EIFFEL TOWER FUN FACTS

1. There are 7,000 metric tons of iron in the structure
2. It's 1050 feet tall — massive!
3. It is lit up at night with 20,000 lightbulbs
4. It was originally built as the entrance for the 1889 World's Fair
5. It is named after Gustav Eiffel. His company built and designed it
6. They started building it in 1887 (only 2 years to complete it!)
7. It's painted brown every 7 years

TRAVEL TIPS

Be sure to reserve tickets for tours well in advance. The Louvre tour is world famous, and it sells out early.

THE LOURVE & THE LEFT BANK

Today you're going to see some famous Parisian art and artifacts that should start to give you a picture of the culture and history. Try to notice what's different from your home country.

- **MORNING:** The Louvre Museum
- **AFTERNOON:** Left Bank & Latin Quarter

 **DAY 3**

 **STOP #1** THE LOUVRE

MORNING: Find your way to the Louvre Museum — let's start with the biggest eyefull of amazing stuff you'll ever see right after breakfast so you're ready to focus!

The Mona Lisa is the most world-famous painting shown at the Louvre. Find out why she is so famous when you get there!

 ST. GERMAIN BOULEVARD FOR LUNCH

STOP #2 BOULEVARD S^T GERMAIN

LUNCH: you're going to need nurishment after taking in the Louvre! It's a big place and you could spend a whole day in there. Walk across the bridge to Left Bank and find lunch somewhere on St. Germain Boulevard on your way to the Latin Quarter.

AFTERNOON: Now you're going to walk a bit to see some indications of what the city was like long before it was called Paris when the Romans were running the city (it was much smaller back then too). One of the things to keep in mind about Europe is it's recorded history goes back really far. Some of the monuments on this tour will look very different from the others surrounding them.

Paris Tour

DAY 3 ➤ **CONTINUED**

DID YOU KNOW? Sorbonne University is in the Latin Quarter. There are lots of students living here.

STOP #3 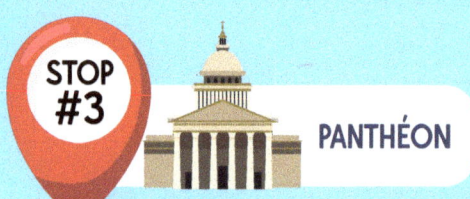 **PANTHÉON**

You've got to walk by or go in depending on how much capacity you have to see more old stuff. The Panthéon holds cultural artifacts and tombs (where important people were buried) for the military back in that day.

ARÈNES DE LUTÈCE **STOP #4**

This first century (that means before the year 100 AD) Roman ampitheatre is hidden from street view in the Latin Quarter. You can walk through it on your way to the Catacomb tour. It's basically a very old Roman theatre. Not much of it is left today, but you'll get the idea.

STOP #5  **CATACOMBS**

If you like this sort of thing, you'll definitely want to take this tour. A top Paris attraction, this is an ancient burial ground with the remains of 6+ million people who died centuries ago!

LATE AFTERNOON: Phew! That stuff was really old but good to know! Summer days are long, so why not take time to recharge before dinner? Make your way to Luxembourg Garden to relax, maybe sail some miniature boats on the lake and enjoy your day the way the Parisians do! Do you see any adults playing petanque? Maybe you'd like to get an ice cream!

 JARDIN (GARDEN) DU LUXEMBOURG

STOP #6

 The chateau has been here since 1612 when the widow of King Henry IV constructed the Luxembourg Palace as her new residence. The palace is owned today by the French Senate (government), which meets there.

DAY 4

 **RIVER CRUISE ON THE SEINE, NOTRE DAME CATHEDRAL AND CHOCOSTORY PARIS!**

I'll bet you are ready to slow down the pace with a little less walking today. Time for a river cruise, a story about a famous cathedral and then fill your senses with French Chocolate!

- **MORNING:** River Seine boat cruise
- **AFTERNOON:** Notre Dame Cathedral, ChocoStory tour!

STOP #1

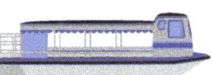 **Morning: HOP-ON, HOP-OFF RIVER CRUISE & NOTRE DAME CATHEDRAL**

 Take the Hop-On, Hop-Off river cruise to eventually hop off at Notre Dame Cathedral. You'll cruise by monuments you'll recognize and see the city from a different view.

Paris Tour

STOP #2

Afternoon:
NORTE DAME

Notre Dame Cathedral was built during medieval times. Remember the Hunchback of Notre Dame book mentioned earlier — you'll get to see where the story takes place up close and personal. Do the tour and learn about why it is visited by 12 million people every year!

STOP #3

Late Afternoon:
CHOCOSTORY TOUR

The ChocoStory Paris tour is a perfect way to end the afternoon with a something delicious. You'll meet the chefs and learn the history of chocolate, see some chocolate art, you'll get to eat some and can even make your own. Parisians love their chocolate and you'll find it in many places.

DID YOU KNOW?

The first chocolate-making factory in Paris opened in 1559. Monsieur Debuisson invented the chocolate-making process by creating a machine to grind cocoa beans making the preparation of chocolate a lot easier.

Also, the French are famous for chocolate truffles. It has a chocolate ganache center and is typically coated in cocoa powder, coconut or chopped nuts. You MUST try one! It will make your tastebuds quite happy. The quality of the ingredients is the best.

Gianduia chocolate was invented during Napoleon's rule (1796-1884) in France and includes 30% hazelnut paste. It's used in many cakes today.

Do you know where most cocoa beans come from? Typically Mexico, Central and South America. They grow on trees!

DAY 5 — **STOP #1** — **DAY TRIP:** THE PALACE OF VERSAILLES

THE PALACE OF VERSAILLES – A DAY IN THE FRENCH COUNTRYSIDE

DAY TRIP: I hope you're well rested today and have extra energy from your chocolate tasting. This palace is one of the most grand in all of France. Very famous kings and queens have lived here over the centuries. If you recall, there is no royal family now in France so it's open to the public and used for grand parties and balls now. The website says it's not just a palace, it's an entire city!

- The Palace was listed as a World Heritage site in 1979 and is considered one of the greatest achievements in French 17th century art
- There are statues, tennis courts, stables, the most grand gardens with fountains you've ever seen, a ballroom and much more
- If you've ever wanted to know what it was like back in that day, the art alone in this palace will give you a visual you'll never forget. It's beyond grand
- It used to be the seat of power but is now a museum of French history.

TRAVEL TIPS — HOW WILL YOU GET THERE?

The Palace is outside of central Paris, about a 1 hour journey. You can organize a tour bus to take you or take public transportation from the center of Paris to get there from, or somewhere near your hotel. You can ask your hotel to arrange it. It's worth all the hassle.

Paris Tour

INTERESTING FACTS ABOUT THE PALACE TOUR:

- The palace has 2,300 rooms. Wait, what? You've got to see it to believe it
- The palace was originally a hunting lodge for Louis XIII (1601-1643)
- There are 372 statues, 600 fountains and 20 miles of water pipes
- Hot chocolate was the drink of choice for King Louis XV (15th). This is my kind of party!

The tour takes 2-3 hours comfortably, so take a snack with you just in case.

DID YOU KNOW?

Napoleon Bonaparte is a very important ruler who took over after the government decided there would be no more kings. He lived at the Palace of Versaille at a very turbulent time following the French Revolution. You'll have to visit a museum to learn more about that. Be on the lookout for a very famous painting of Napoleon on his horse by Jaques-Louis-David created in 1801. It is said he was a very short but very powerful man.

FUN FACTS!

In the beginning of the renaissance period (1400s), the term "chateau" was used to refer to the rural location of a luxurious residence as opposed to an urban palace. Today we can call it a palace.

French royalty, notably Kings, are identified with Roman numerals. Apparently their first names repeated from father to son, for many generations. For example Louis XIV (14th) created Versailles chateau from a village of the same name that was destroyed back in 1673. His father's name was Louis XIII (13th) as you might expect.

King Louis XIV

DAY 6

DAY TRIP: DISNEYLAND

Oui, S'il vous plait!
That means Yes, please!
(pronounced "we, see voo-play!")

You can't come all the way to Paris and not do Disneyland if you've never been.

TRAVEL TIPS

How will I get there? From Central Paris you'll need to board a train or take a tour bus.

There is some travel time to getting to Disneyland outside of Paris, but it's doable for the day. If you're flying out the next day (Day 7) you'll want ot come back and relax before you pack up. You have the option of staying at or near Disneyland too if it makes sense.

I could go on and on about what to do there but there is a website, so make sure you visit it as soon as possible. Tickets are in high demand. Don't miss out!

Paris Tour

TRAVEL DAY TO YOUR NEXT DESTINATION

DAY 7

Typically on your last day in Paris, you'll be getting ready to travel home or to your next destination. If you have extra time, include something else fun in your plans — that could just be shopping or finding your favorite cafe to sit and enjoy watching people! Otherwise, bonjour and bonne-chance ("bun-shance" means good luck)!

PLANNING YOUR TRIP

Your tour could look much different from this, depending on when you can get your tickets. Or perhaps you will decide you're not that interested in something. Make sure you plan carefully in the planning section of this book on pages 57 and 58.

TRAVEL TIPS

Remember to add airport transit time to your travel plans. If you're flying out of Paris, it takes time to pack, eat, and get to an airport in a big city. And you've got to be there at least 2 hours before the flight. It's fastest to take the Metro! You can avoid all the traffic but that means you have to carry all your luggage with you.

IDEAS FOR THINGS TO DO IN A MORNING OR AFTERNOON:

- Atelier des Lumières — a digital immersive exhibition
- Jardin du Luxembourg (see page 41 of the tour)
- Sacre Coeur on Montmarte hill
- Virtual arial tour of Paris (see flyview360.com/en)
- Notre Dame Virtual Reality (VR) tour
- Shakespeare and Company bookstore — Latin Quarter

Andrew & Ashley's
EUROPEAN TOURS

TEST YOUR KNOWLEDGE WITH ACTIVITIES!

Now that you've learned a lot about Paris, let's test your memory and have a little fun. Remember, you can always go back to find the answers in the main part of the book.

PARIS & FRANCE

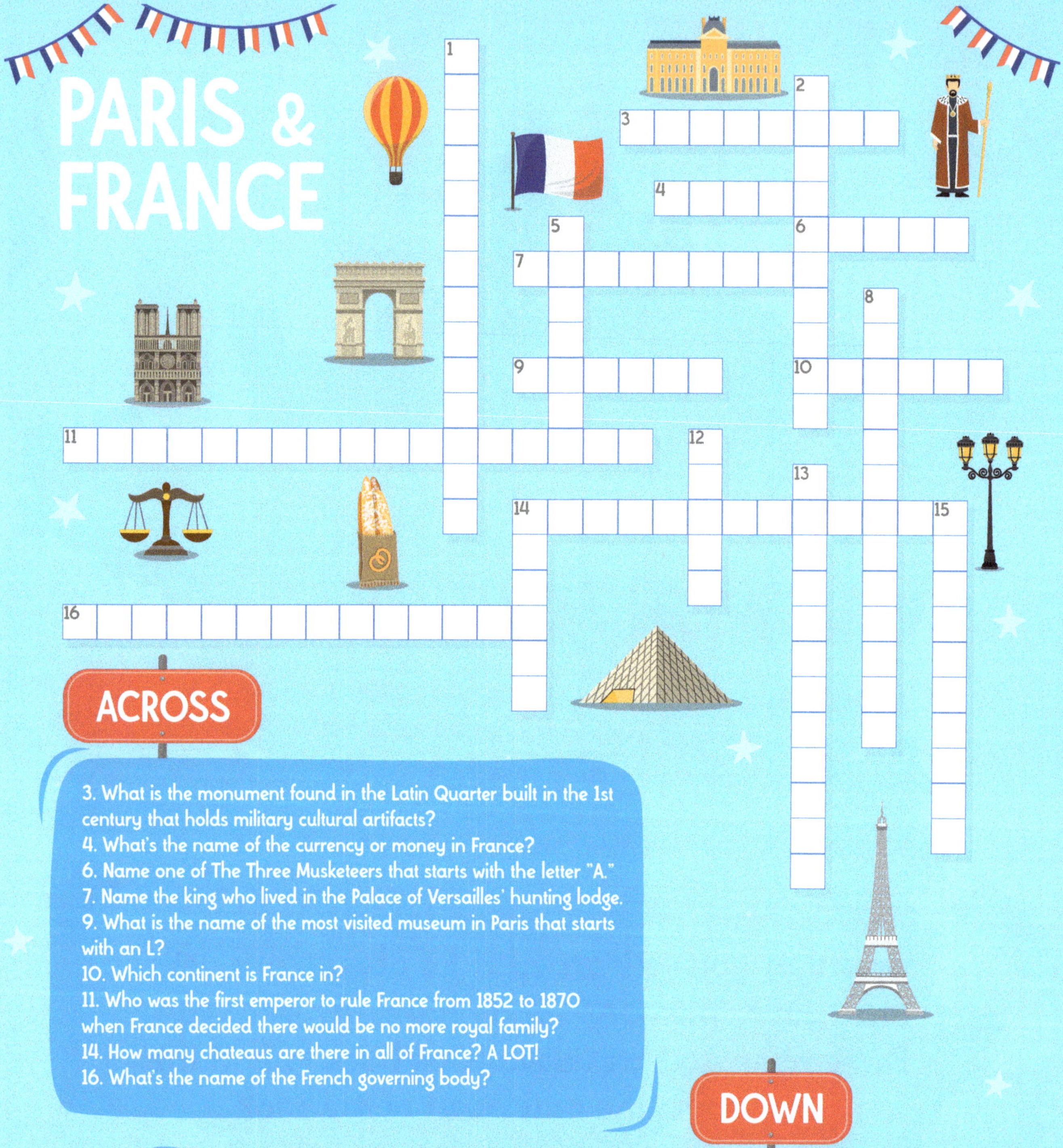

ACROSS

3. What is the monument found in the Latin Quarter built in the 1st century that holds military cultural artifacts?
4. What's the name of the currency or money in France?
6. Name one of The Three Musketeers that starts with the letter "A."
7. Name the king who lived in the Palace of Versailles' hunting lodge.
9. What is the name of the most visited museum in Paris that starts with an L?
10. Which continent is France in?
11. Who was the first emperor to rule France from 1852 to 1870 when France decided there would be no more royal family?
14. How many chateaus are there in all of France? A LOT!
16. What's the name of the French governing body?

DOWN

1. How many lightbulbs does the Eiffel Tower have?
2. What is the name of the palace just outside Paris where Louis XIV once lived?
5. How do you say hello (during the day) in France?
8. What's the name of the European governing body that France is part of?
12. What's the name of the underground train that runs throughout Paris?
13. What is the oldest monument in Paris?
14. What country is Paris in?
15. Name a world famous adventure park just outside of Paris.

PARIS & FRANCE

ACROSS

2. What do you call a street performer that wears white makeup on his or her face and mimics people's movements?
4. What is THE most popular sport in France — that we sometimes call soccer?
6. What color is the Eiffel tower painted every year?
7. What is the name of the person who used to entertain the courts?
9. What do you call a small restaurant that is typically family owned and passed down from generation to generation?
10. Who are the famous swordsmen who fought for justice?
11. What is like a very thin pancake that is served in a crêperie?
13. What is the most famous painting at the Louvre museum?
14. What is the name of the famous French children's song that sings of brother John sleeping? (Frère means brother, and Jaques is John in English!)
15. What is the name of the young star footballer who is ranked 3rd in France?
16. What is the name of the famous cycle race that starts and ends in France?
17. What is the phrase that describes Paris because the city sparkles at night?
18. What do you call a bakery in France?
19. Name a famous painting that Vincent Van Gogh painted.
20. The original, called Le Chat Botte, is a French book turned into a Dreamworks animated film called _____.

DOWN

1. Name the famous musical that is played around the world that translates to "The Miserables" in English.
3. Whats the title for someone in the hotel that can help you get around the city of Paris?
5. What is the world's most famous French pastry?
8. What is the side of the river called where the Latin Quarter and Luxembourg Garden are?
12. Name a famous Italian painter that painted the Mona Lisa.

THE MAZE TO ARC DE TRIOMPHE!

START HERE

THE MAZE TO NOTRE DAME!

START HERE

PARIS CULTURE

```
L Y A R C D E T R I O M P H E Y X E
R C R E P E I S A C R E C O E U R I
P O K E F H R J M H Q O A B G P R F
O L Y X F B V R J R A V Q P P C B F
O Y K T A U R E V O I R R Y B J K E
D M B R E A M I C K E Y M O U S E L
L P Q I Y W Z Y N O T R E D A M E T
E I P A I N A U C H O C O L A T E O
I C J S E I N E E B A G U E T T E W
V S U H O T C H O C O L A T E K D E
Z Q V V G C D A C H E E S E D C D R
C R O Q U E M O N S I E U R D G R D
```

Find the following words in the puzzle.
Words are hidden → ↓ and ↘.

ARC DE TRIOMPHE
AU REVOIR
BAGUETTE
CHEESE
CREPE

CROQUE MONSIEUR
EIFFEL TOWER
HOT CHOCOLATE
MICKEY MOUSE
NOTRE DAME

OLYMPICS
PAIN AU CHOCOLAT
POODLE
SACRE COEUR
SEINE

FILL IN THE BLANKS

ENGLISH TO FRENCH WORDS & PHRASES

See if you can write out the French words with the grammatical accents shown in the table on page 29.

1. How do you say hello to a woman during the evening in France? Bonsoir Madame. And if it's a man? _____ _____

2. If you want to ask someone if they speak English, how do you say it in French? _____ _____

3. You want to introduce yourself to a French person, how do you say "my name is:" Je _____ _____.

4. How do you say thank you in French? _____

5. If someone asks you how you are by saying "comment ca va," what do you say? _____ _____ (good, thank you)

6. When an adult asks for the check after a nice lunch, how should they request it? _____ _____ _____ _____ (the check please!)

7. You want to buy something in a market, how do you ask "how much" it is? _____ _____?

8. What if you have just tasted something really good, how would you say wow! ___ ___ ___

9. How do you ask someone how they are? _____ ___ ___

10. When you're in the park and you see a small dog, what do you call it? Le _____ _____ (a small dog)

11. You meet some people in your travels who are French. How say "have a nice weekend" in French to them as you depart? _____ _____

12. You are sitting in a restaurant and you see a woman pick up her cell phone and say this: _____ _____! What does it mean? _____.

13. If you want to ask for something in a shop, how do you say "I would like a croissant?" ___ _____ un _____.

14. You are leaving your hotel and want to say goodbye to the front desk people but you are returning later. How do you say "good bye and see you later" in French? ___ _____ et ___ _____!

15. How do you say "have a nice day" (this was mentioned in the book but is not on page 29) _____ _____.

Make sure you practice a few of these phrases using the pronounciations shown on page 29. And don't forget you can also use a translate app to look up what you want to say too. It will tell you what it sounds like to say it. It's fun to try when you're in Paris!

Who We Met in Paris on Our Last Trip!

DID YOU KNOW?

The **French Poodle** comes in four sizes: Standard, Medium, Miniature and Toy. **Coco** — a girl - is a toy Poodle, so the smallest one. She is the perfect size for an apartment in the city. They have a thick, curly coat mostly in solid colors like white, black, brown, grey and apricot — like Coco's. Poodles are active and intelligent and able to learn more than most dogs from their humans.

We decided one sunny afternoon, during our trip, to visit **Luxembourg Garden**. There, we met other kids our age sailing small sailboats in the lake. They asked us if we wanted to join in and the adults got each of us a small model sailboat to try. It was super fun.

Hi, our names are **Charlotte and Tristan. Welcome to Paris!** These are our dogs Coco and Beau! Isn't this park amazing?

The **French Bulldog** breed, known for their distinctive bat-like ears is. In earlier days they were highly sought after by society ladies, artists, writers, and fashion designers — but now is a common family dog. **Beau** is a boy — and he's very funny! They are said to be patient, affectionate and need close companionship with their humans.

PLAN YOUR FAMILY TRIP

DAY #1 — Travel day plus something fun!

FIRST DAY: I ARRIVE.

My flight arrives on this date _____ time _____

It will take me ____ hour(s) to get to my hotel.

We will take _____ transportation to get to our hotel.

It will take us ____ hours to get settled in the hotel.

How many hours do I have left in the day to do something? _____

Where will we go later in the day? _____

We are planning a trip to Paris!

DAY #2	LOCATION	TRANSPORT TO THE NEXT STOP
Morning	_____	_____
Lunch	_____	_____
Afternoon	_____	_____
Dinner	_____	_____
Evening	_____	_____

TRAVEL TIPS

Don't forget to have breakfast in the morning before you set out!

DAY #3	LOCATION	TRANSPORT TO THE NEXT STOP
Morning	_____	_____
Lunch	_____	_____
Afternoon	_____	_____
Dinner	_____	_____
Evening	_____	_____

DAY #4	LOCATION	TRANSPORT TO THE NEXT STOP
Morning	_____	_____
Lunch	_____	_____
Afternoon	_____	_____
Dinner	_____	_____
Evening	_____	_____

DAY #5	LOCATION	TRANSPORT TO THE NEXT STOP
Morning	_____	_____
Lunch	_____	_____
Afternoon	_____	_____
Dinner	_____	_____
Evening	_____	_____

DAY #6	LOCATION	TRANSPORT TO THE NEXT STOP
Morning	_____	_____
Lunch	_____	_____
Afternoon	_____	_____
Dinner	_____	_____
Evening	_____	_____

DAY #7

LAST DAY

My flight departs on this date _____ time:_____

It will take me ____ hour(s) to get from my hotel to the airport.

We will take the _____ (transportation) to get to the airport.

We would have to leave at _____ to arrive at the airport 2 hours before our flight.

Do I have time to do something fun before going to the airport? _____

Where will we go if we have time? _____

Andrew & Ashley's
EUROPEAN TOURS

GET THE PARIS 2024 SUMMER OLYMPICS JOURNAL!

Get fun facts and track your favorite competitions!

Visit **AndrewandAshleysEuropeanTours.com** for more travel details, additional activities, updates on travel destinations, and more.

AU REVOIR ET BONNE SOIRÉE! GOODBYE AND HAVE A NICE EVENING!

We've had some incredible experiences and seen so many new things in Paris so far. This visit is just the beginning! There is so much more to see in France and around Europe. We hope you take advantage of every minute in Paris to learn and try as many new things as you can, because who knows? You may want to come back someday as an exchange student or on an epic trip with your friends!

So à bientôt! Until next time.